CAPOEiRA

Game! Dance! Martial Art!

George Ancona

Lee & Low Books Inc. ◉ New York

Acknowledgments

This book would have been impossible to produce without the kindness and generosity of the many people who offered help, advice, knowledge, and enthusiasm. Thanks to Mestre Marcelo; Malandro, Cipó, Sumido, Indio, Bengala, and the other instructors; and the students and families of Mandinga Academy in Oakland, California. In Brazil, to Sací of Filhos de Bimba; to Lia Robatto of Projeto Axé; to Harmonía, Mestre Renê, and Gui Alcântara; and to Mestre Rio Cheio. To Mestre Acordeon in Berkeley, California, and to Mestre Amen in Los Angeles, California. To Pete Jackson in Santa Fe, New Mexico. To Mestre João Grande and Mestre Ombrinho in New York City. To Richard and Sandra Graham. To Celia Pederson; my daughters, Gina, Lisa, and Marina; and my wife, Helga, who smoothed the path through the intricacies of Portuguese.

Muito obrigado! Many thanks!   —G.A.

Drawings on pages 18, 28, and 31 by George Ancona, based on old photographs. Drawing on page 30 by George Ancona, based on a lithograph by João Maurício Rugendas. Lithograph on page 29 by João Maurício Rugendas, courtesy of Helga von Sydow.

LEE & LOW BOOKS Inc., 95 Madison Avenue, New York, NY 10016
leeandlow.com

Manufactured in China

Book design by David and Susan Neuhaus/NeuStudio
Book production by The Kids at Our House

The text is set in Berkeley Book
10 9 8 7 6 5 4 3 2 1
First Edition

Library of Congress Cataloging-in-Publication Data
Ancona, George.
　　Capoeira : game! dance! martial art! / George Ancona. — 1st ed.
　　p. cm.
Summary: "Photo-essay about Capoeira, a game, dance, and martial art, as it is played in the United States and Brazil today, plus its history and origins in the African slave culture of Brazil during the seventeenth century. Includes a glossary of Portuguese words and Web sources"—Provided by publisher.
ISBN 978-1-58430-268-1
1. Capoeira (Dance)—Juvenile literature. I. Title.
GV1796.C145A53 2007
793.3'1981—dc22   2006028866

To Helga

CAPOEIRA—it's a game, a dance, a martial art! For those who play capoeira, it is a way of life.

The first time I saw capoeira I was in Salvador, Bahia, the old capital of Brazil. A crowd surrounded a circle of young men who sang and played strange-looking instruments. Suddenly two men cartwheeled into the middle of the circle and began to lash out with lightning kicks. They spun on their heads, ducked, and dove over each other, yet they never touched. When they stopped, drenched with sweat, they hugged and laughed. This experience sparked my curiosity, and I began to explore capoeira in both Brazil and the United States.

George Ancona

Many of the words used in capoeira are Portuguese, the language spoken in Brazil.
Pronunciations and meanings of the Portuguese words are given at the back of the book.

Today capoeira is played around the world. It has become popular because it is challenging and fun. It also allows boys and girls, men and women to express themselves through movement, music, and *malícia*, the trickery used in capoeira.

Capoeira schools, called academies, are found all across the United States. In Oakland, California, children go to Mandinga Academy to learn capoeira. Classes begin with stretches that prepare the students' bodies for the movements of the game. These moves are the tools the students will use to play capoeira without hurting each other.

Legends tell us that capoeira was created by African slaves who were brought to Brazil starting in the sixteenth century. In the late nineteenth century capoeira was declared illegal by the government. So the *capoeiristas*, people who fought using capoeira, had to practice in secret, and they used nicknames to hide their true identities. In 1930 capoeira was once again permitted, as a martial art and game.

Today capoeiristas still use Portuguese—the language spoken in Brazil—for their nicknames. These students at Mandinga Academy are called:

Cajú (cashew)

Elástica (elastic)

Fogo (fire)

Reizinho (little king)

Astronauta (astronaut)

Coringa (joker)

Perereca (tree frog)

Catatau (shorty)

Maravilha (amazing)

Pingüim (penguin)

Malvado (mean)

Princesa (princess)

Chocolate (chocolate)

Their instructor is called
Malandro (scoundrel).

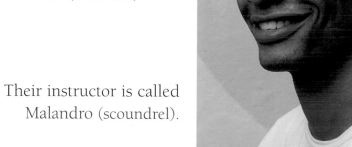

ponte (bridge)

espelho (mirror)

Capoeira has many different moves that are used for attack and defense. Each move has a name, such as *ponte* (bridge), *espelho* (mirror), and *parafuso* (twist). Some moves, including *caranguejo* (crab), *gato* (cat), and *macaco* (monkey), imitate the movements of animals.

Capoeira combines dance, music, and acrobatics with fighting techniques. While playing, capoeiristas touch the floor only with their hands and feet. They may also touch the floor with their heads.

parafuso (twist)

caranguejo (crab)

Perereca demonstrates a *ginga*, the basic moves that begin a game. The ginga is a springboard for the many movements that follow.

When two players start a game they face each other and step from side to side and forward and back in a kind of dance. This gives each player a chance to size up his or her opponent. Then the players begin to exchange movements of attack and defense. The object of the game is to put one's opponent in a position where he or she could be taken down with a sweep, kick, or blow. The players do not actually hit each other. Showing how an opponent might be taken down or pretending to strike is more impressive than actually doing it.

Chocolate demonstrates a *meia lua de compasso*, an arching kick that is used to attack from the ground. Maravilha squats and protects her head in a defensive move called the *cocorinha*.

ginga (side-to-side, forward-and-back moves)

meia lua de compasso
(arching kick)

cocorinha

(squatting below
a kick)

rasteira (sweep kick)

aú (cartwheel)

aú with *rasteira*

Reizinho drops to the ground in a defensive position called the *rasteira*, which becomes an attack with a sweeping movement to the opponent's foot. This is how he could trip or take down Perereca as she moves through an *aú*, a cartwheel. Malandro demonstrates an attack with a front kick called a *benção*.

Capoeiristas are playful and respectful as they move in continuous sequences from attack to defense and back to attack. The sequences take place smoothly, unexpectedly, and to the rhythm of the music. Each player must try to guess his or her opponent's moves and be ready to attack or defend.

During a game the players never take their eyes off each other. Malandro tells his students they must play as if they have eight eyes around their heads, always aware of what is happening.

benção (front kick)

Sometimes Malandro gathers the class together to teach his students a new song in Portuguese. He begins by playing a rhythm on a *pandeiro*, a tambourine. First he teaches his students the chorus. Then he sings one line of the song. Everybody responds by clapping and singing the chorus.

Capoeira songs are about Brazil, its people and history, the sea, gods and goddesses, myths, capoeira, and the players themselves.

pandeiro

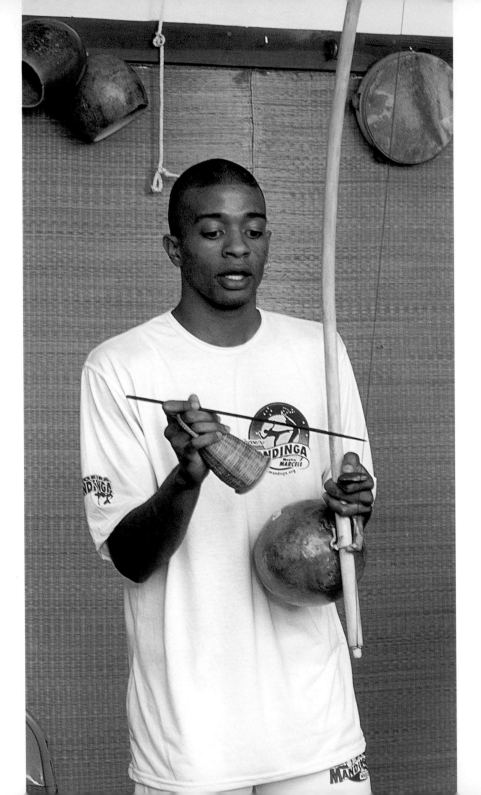

After teaching his students the song, Malandro begins to play an instrument called a *berimbau*. The berimbau is a long wood bow with a steel wire and a hollowed-out gourd near the bottom. The instrument is held with the left hand, which also holds a coin or stone. The right hand holds a small rattle and a stick with which to hit the wire to produce a buzzing sound. The coin or stone is moved back and forth from the wire to change the pitch of the sound.

The berimbau is used to direct the capoeira games. Its music tells the capoeiristas what kind of game to play— fast, slow, playful, or aggressive.

In nineteenth-century Brazil berimbaus were also used by peddlers to announce their arrival in town.

berimbau

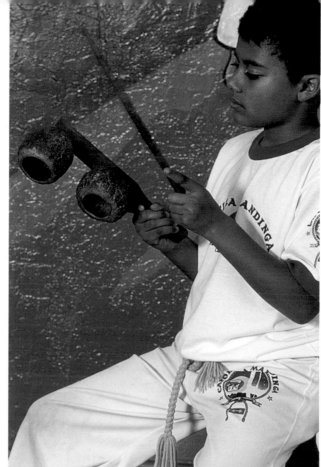

réco-réco

atabaque

agogô

Another instrument used in capoeira is the *atabaque*, a tall drum. The *agogô* is made of two coconut shells or cowbells mounted together. They are hit with a stick, and each shell or bell produces a different tone. The *réco-réco* is a piece of bamboo cut with notches. It is played by moving a stick up and down the notches to make a rasping sound.

Together the music, singing, and clapping set the rhythm and style for the games the capoeiristas play.

Malandro's class is sometimes joined by Marcelo, Mandinga Academy's *mestre,* or master, and the other instructors. The group is like a family. Mestre Marcelo is the father figure and the instructors are the older brothers and sisters.

Everyone forms a *roda,* a circle. Some of the instructors and students choose instruments and join the master. Mestre Marcelo begins playing his berimbau to start the game. Two players crouch in front of him and hold hands. After the mestre tips his berimbau over the players, they cartwheel into the center of the roda and begin to play.

Each player starts with a ginga and then goes into acrobatic sequences. They play with speed, instinct, and malícia, the trickery that is important to the game. The players have fun and try to make their moves graceful, like a dance. They also try to keep their white clothes clean by not getting taken down.

The berimbaus stop and the players give each other an *abraço,* a hug. They return to the roda and two new players cartwheel into the center. They are encouraged by the pounding music, the songs, and the rhythmic clapping, which turns into applause when a beautiful move is made.

There is no need to match players evenly. Skill and cunning are more important than age, size, or weight. Games may be played between boys and women, men and girls. Some games may be played harder, as more advanced players try to take each other down.

Instructors play with the mestre to improve their skills. Malandro first plays with Mestre Marcelo, then with Cipó, another instructor.

In many cities instructors go out to neighborhood schools to introduce students to capoeira. Cipó brings his pandeiro and berimbau to a school in Oakland's Chinatown. The children sing along as Cipó plays the pandeiro. Then they form a roda and practice basic moves to the rhythm of the berimbau.

During these classes the children discover the thrill of playing capoeira. They become familiar with the music, songs, acrobatic moves, and trickery that are all part of the game. And they have fun!

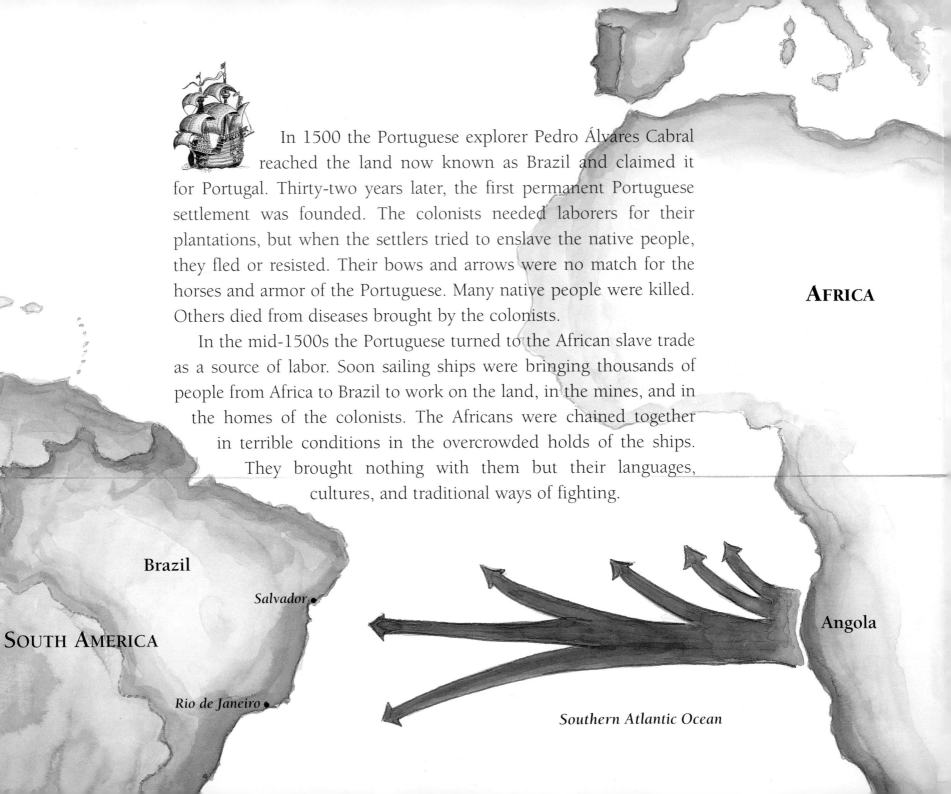

In 1500 the Portuguese explorer Pedro Álvares Cabral reached the land now known as Brazil and claimed it for Portugal. Thirty-two years later, the first permanent Portuguese settlement was founded. The colonists needed laborers for their plantations, but when the settlers tried to enslave the native people, they fled or resisted. Their bows and arrows were no match for the horses and armor of the Portuguese. Many native people were killed. Others died from diseases brought by the colonists.

In the mid-1500s the Portuguese turned to the African slave trade as a source of labor. Soon sailing ships were bringing thousands of people from Africa to Brazil to work on the land, in the mines, and in the homes of the colonists. The Africans were chained together in terrible conditions in the overcrowded holds of the ships. They brought nothing with them but their languages, cultures, and traditional ways of fighting.

AFRICA

Brazil

Salvador

SOUTH AMERICA

Rio de Janeiro

Angola

Southern Atlantic Ocean

Slave market in Rio de Janeiro, Brazil

The owners felt threatened by their slaves' fighting skills, so they forbade them to practice. The slaves then disguised their fights with music to trick their owners into thinking they were dancing.

Some slaves managed to escape to remote areas and formed settlements called *quilombos*. Traditional fighting was refined there and developed into what is now capoeira. After the abolition of slavery, the freed slaves headed to the cities. There was little work, and some of the men formed gangs that used capoeira. As a result, the government outlawed capoeira around 1890. Many capoeiristas were arrested. In 1930 the ban was lifted, and the playing of capoeira as a Brazilian martial art and game was allowed.

Street capoeira

Mestre Bimba (Manoel dos Reis Machado) was a great capoeirista and berimbau musician. He was born in 1900 in Salvador, a city on the northeast coast of Brazil. His father taught him to fight in the African way, and a sea captain taught him capoeira. Bimba later created many moves and sequences of blows. In 1932, after capoeira became legal, Mestre Bimba opened the first officially-recognized academy. His style became known as Capoeira Regional. It is a modern, upright style played to a fast rhythm. Mestre Bimba died in 1974.

Mestre Bimba

Mestre Pastinha (Vicente Ferreira Pastinha) was also born in Salvador, in 1889. As a boy he was bullied by a bigger child. His neighbor, an African man from Angola, saw this and taught little Vicente how to fight. In 1942 Mestre Pastinha started his own academy to teach the traditional style of capoeira called Capoeira Angola. It is played more slowly and closer to the ground than Capoeira Regional. Mestre Pastinha also wrote a book and many songs about capoeira. He died in 1981.

Mestre Bimba and Mestre Pastinha are considered the fathers of today's capoeira.

Mestre Pastinha

Capoeira continues to change. The two styles—Capoeira Regional and Capoeira Angola—often mix in a style known as Capoeira Contemporânea. In Brazil students choose the academy where they train based on the style taught by the mestre. Children also play capoeira on streets, beaches, or anyplace they find a friend. This was how people learned capoeira before academies existed.

Many community centers and churches in Brazil offer free capoeira classes for children and teenagers. In a classroom of a church school in Salvador, Harmonía teaches Capoeira Regional to girls and boys in the mornings. The children begin by stretching and practicing their moves. Harmonía helps the youngest players learn the movements correctly. Then the children pair up and play games of capoeira with each other.

In the afternoons Mestre René teaches Capoeira Angola to teenagers. The master and some of the students choose their instruments while others warm up for the games. Then everyone forms a roda and the play begins.

The young men and women in Mestre René's classes are skillful players. The games are played close to the ground, and the players' powerful moves are controlled and graceful.

Mestre René holds Capoeira Angola games in his academy in the evenings. These events are called *rodas*. Mestre René and several of the players like to wear their hair in dreadlocks. To keep their long hair out of the way, they wrap white cloths around their heads.

Capoeiristas of different ages often play together. When a player is tired he may spread out his arms in a move called a *chamada*. His opponent places her hand on his shoulder and they walk back and forth until the first player begins to play again. But the opponent must be careful. The chamada may be a trick, and the first player might strike out with a sudden attack, catching his opponent off guard.

Like many capoeira instructors in the United States, Malandro often goes to Brazil to study and train. Malandro and some of the other instructors also visit schools in the neighborhoods of Salvador. There they teach capoeira and play games with the children. With their strength, skills, and discipline, the instructors are positive role models. The children learn the value of education, training, and respect for their elders.

Back in Oakland, California, the students and instructors at Mandinga Academy celebrate the end of the school year with a ceremony called a *batizado*. Mestre Marcelo invites masters from near and far to join in the celebration. Families and friends come too. Everyone is there to watch the students show their skills as capoeiristas.

Students wear yellow T-shirts. Instructors and mestres wear blue. Mestre Marcelo sets the pace and rhythm of the games with the music of his berimbau. Every student must play with a master or an instructor. Each game ends with a roar of applause.

At the end of a game the student gets an abraço from his or her instructor and receives a *cordão*, a colored rope. The colors of the cordãos are those of the Brazilian flag. Green is for the beginners. Yellow is for the next level up. Then comes blue. Braided color combinations are for in-between levels. Instructors wear blue cordãos, and mestres wear white.

Mestre Marcelo and the instructors are proud of their students, and the students look forward to continuing to improve their skills as capoeiristas. They will have fun as they find new ways to express themselves through the game, dance, and martial art of capoeira.

Glossary and Pronunciation Guide

Pronunciations of some Portuguese words vary from region to region within Brazil.
The pronunciations below reflect the language as spoken around the city of Salvador.

abraço (ah-BRAH-so): hug, embrace

agogô (ah-goh-GUH): instrument made of two cowbells
or coconut shells mounted together

Angola (an-GOH-lah): country of southwest
Africa bordering the Atlantic Ocean

astronauta (as-troh-NOW-tah): astronaut

atabaque (ah-tah-BAH-keh): tall drum

aú (ah-OO): cartwheel; capoeira move

Bahia (bah-EE-ah): northeastern Brazilian state

batizado (bah-tee-ZAH-doh): baptism,
initiation ceremony

benção (BEN-saow): front kick; capoeira attack move

berimbau (beh-reem-BAU): instrument
consisting of wood bow strung with steel wire,
and hollow gourd

cajú (kah-JOO): cashew

capoeira (kah-poo-AY-rah): Brazilian game, dance, and
martial art

capoeirista (kah-poo-ay-RIS-tah): person who plays capoeira

caranguejo (kah-ran-GAY-joo): crab; capoeira move

catatau (kah-tah-TAH-oo): shorty

chamada (shah-MAH-dah): call; capoeira trick move

chocolate (sho-koh-LAH-teh): chocolate

cipó (see-POH): vine

cocorinha (koh-koh-REE-nya): squatting movement;
capoeira defensive move

contemporânea (kon-tem-poh-RUH-nee-ah): contemporary

cordão (kor-DAUN): cord, rope

coringa (kor-REEN-gah): joker

elástica (eh-LAS-tee-kah): elastic

espelho (ess-PEH-lee-oh): mirror; capoeira move

fogo (FOH-goh): fire

gato (GAH-toh): cat; capoeira move

ginga (JEEN-gah): side-to-side, forward-and-back movements;
capoeira moves that begin a game

harmonía (ar-moh-NEE-ah): harmony

macaco (mah-KAH-koh): monkey; capoeria move

malandro (mah-LAN-droh): scoundrel

malícia (mah-LEE-see-ah): cunning, trickery

malvado (mahl-VAH-doh): mean

mandinga (man-DEEN-gah): witchcraft

Manoel dos Reis Machado (mah-nu-EH-oo dos hey-ESS
mah-SHAH-doh): founder of Capoeira Regional

maravilha (mah-rah-VEE-lee-ah): amazing

meia lua de compasso (MAY-yah LOO-ah deh com-PAH-soh):
arching kick; capoeira attack move from the ground

mestre (MESS-tree): master

pandeiro (pahn-DAY-roh): tambourine

parafuso (pah-rah-FU-zoh): twist; capoeira move

Pedro Álvares Cabral (PEH-droh AL-vah-res
kah-BRAU): Portuguese explorer who
claimed Brazil for Portugal in 1500

pererecа (peh-reh-REH-kah): tree frog

pingüim (peen-GWEEN): penguin

ponte (PON-teh): bridge; capoeira move

princesa (preen-SEH-zah): princess

quilombo (kee-LOM-boh): Brazilian slave
settlement

rasteira (has-TAY-rah): low sweep kick;
capoeira defensive move

réco-réco (HEH-koh-HEH-koh): instrument made of bamboo cut with notches

reizinho (hey-ZEE-nyo): little king

regional (heh-jee-oh-NAU): regional

Rio de Janeiro (HEE-oh deh jah-NAY-roh): city on southeastern coast of Brazil

roda (HOH-dah): circle; gathering or event where capoeira is played

Salvador (sal-vah-DOR): city on northeastern coast of Brazil; capital of Bahia

Vicente Ferreira Pastinha (vee-SEN-tee feh-HAY-rah pas-TEE-nya): founder of Capoeira Angola

Find Out More About Capoeira

A search on the Internet will bring up many Web sites with more information about capoeira. Here are some sites that also list capoeira academies in the United States.

Capoeira Online
capoeira.com/news.php

Capoeirista.com
capoeirista.com/schools.php

International Capoeira Angola Foundation
capoeira-angola.org

Planet Capoeira
planetcapoeira.com/pmwiki/pmwiki.php?n=Capoeira.Academies

United Capoeira Association
capoeira.bz

Author's Sources

Almeida, Bira (Mestre Acordeon). *Capoeira, a Brazilian Art Form: History, Philosophy, and Practice.* Berkeley, CA: North Atlantic Books, 1986.

Atwood, Jane. *Capoeira: A Martial Art and a Cultural Tradition.* New York: Rosen Publishing Group, 1999.

Capoeira, Nestor. *Capoeira: Pequeno Manual do Jogador.* Rio de Janeiro: Editora Record, 1998.

———. *The Little Capoeira Book.* Berkeley, CA: North Atlantic Books, 2003.

———. *Roots of the Dance-Fight-Game.* Berkeley, CA: North Atlantic Books, 2002.

Diener, Pablo, and Maria de Fátima Costa. *Rugendas e o Brasil.* São Paulo: Editora Capivara, 2002.

Ermakoff, George. *O Negro na Fotografia Brasileira do Século XIX.* Rio de Janeiro: G. Ermakoff Casa Editorial, 2004.